ELK GROVE VILLAGE PUBLIC LIBRARY
1001 WELLINGTON AVE.
ELK GROVE VILLAGE, IL 60007
(847) 439-0447

SPACE
CRUSADERS

Wernher von Braun

Revolutionary Rocket Engineer

Rachael L. Thomas

Checkerboard
Library

An Imprint of Abdo Publishing
abdobooks.com

ABDOBOOKS.COM

Published by Abdo Publishing, a division of ABDO, PO Box 398166, Minneapolis, Minnesota 55439.
Copyright © 2019 by Abdo Consulting Group, Inc. International copyrights reserved in all countries.
No part of this book may be reproduced in any form without written permission from the publisher.
Checkerboard Library™ is a trademark and logo of Abdo Publishing.

Printed in the United States of America, North Mankato, Minnesota
102018
012019

THIS BOOK CONTAINS RECYCLED MATERIALS

Design: Kelly Doudna, Mighty Media, Inc.
Production: Mighty Media, Inc.
Editor: Rebecca Felix
Front Cover Photographs: NASA (both)
Back Cover Photographs: NASA (Aldrin, ISS, space shuttle, Apollo rocket), Shutterstock (planets)
Interior Photographs: Aelfwine/Wikimedia Commons, pp. 11, 28 (top); AP Images, pp. 15, 29 (bottom);
Daphne Weld Nichols/Wikimedia Commons, p. 25 (bottom left); Getty Images, p. 13; NASA, pp. 5, 16–17, 19, 21,
25 (top left, bottom right), 28 (top, bottom), 29 (top); NASA on The Commons/Flickr, pp. 7, 23; NASA/MSFC, p. 27;
T0501st/Wikimedia Commons, pp. 9, 25 (top right)

Library of Congress Control Number: 2018948531

Publisher's Cataloging-in-Publication Data
Names: Thomas, Rachael L., author.
Title: Wernher von Braun: revolutionary rocket engineer / by Rachael L. Thomas.
Other title: Revolutionary rocket engineer
Description: Minneapolis, Minnesota : Abdo Publishing, 2019 | Series: Space
    crusaders | Includes online resources and index.
Identifiers: ISBN 9781532117060 (lib. bdg.) | ISBN 9781532159909 (ebook)
Subjects: LCSH: Von Braun, Wernher, 1912-1977--Juvenile literature. | Aerospace
    engineers--United States--Biography--Juvenile literature. | Apollo 1
    (Spacecraft)--Juvenile literature. | Rocket ships--Juvenile literature.
Classification: DDC 629.450 [B]--dc23

Contents

Reaching the Stars

Wernher von Braun was a well-known rocket engineer. Originally from Germany, he became a US citizen in 1955. He worked alongside American scientists during the country's efforts to travel to space in the 1950s and 1960s.

Von Braun was a master in his field. He oversaw the development of the rockets that launched the first US **satellite** and the first US astronaut into space. He is best known for leading the development of the *Saturn V* rocket. In 1969, this rocket took humans to the moon for the first time in history!

Many consider von Braun to be a father of modern rocketry. Today's space missions might not have been possible without him! Though von Braun had many great accomplishments, his history is **controversial**. In addition to manufacturing space rockets, he also helped develop deadly weapons for **Nazi** Germany during **World War II**.

Von Braun's creations were not always used for good. But those later in life helped spur space exploration. Von Braun was ambitious and committed to fulfilling his goals. With his help, US astronauts blazed trails in space.

Early Influences

Wernher von Braun was born on March 23, 1912, in Wirsitz, Germany. He was the second of three sons. The von Brauns were wealthy and part of the Lutheran church. When Wernher was **confirmed** in the church, his mother bought him a telescope as a gift.

As Wernher observed the skies through his telescope, he grew fascinated with space. In 1924, 12-year-old Wernher staged his first rocket experiment. He tied store-bought fireworks to his family's wagon and lit them. The fireworks exploded, **propelling** the wagon down the street with Wernher on it!

One year later, Wernher was sent to **boarding school** in central Germany. There, *The Rocket into **Interplanetary** Space* caught his attention. German scientist Hermann Oberth wrote this book. It further inspired Wernher's interest in space.

Oberth's book influenced Wernher in another way too. Wernher was **frustrated** that he did not understand the mathematics used by Oberth. So, Wernher worked hard at school to master math. He had previously struggled with this subject. But Wernher was soon the best in his class!

Von Braun (*second from right*) would later serve on the US Army Ballistic Missile Agency with his idol Hermann Oberth (*center*).

3 Scientists and School

Von Braun graduated high school at age 17. He achieved excellent grades in math and **physics**. In 1930, he **enrolled** at the Berlin Institute of **Technology** to study engineering.

Oberth's books remained influential to von Braun during college. When von Braun was 18, he learned Oberth was traveling near Berlin to conduct experiments with other scientists. Von Braun arranged to meet the scientists. He volunteered to help them with their experiments in his free time.

Von Braun ending up playing a key role among these scientists. Germany's economy was unstable at the time. So, the scientists spent a lot of time requesting **grants** from high-ranking officials to fund rocket experiments. Von Braun made a good impression when speaking with these officials.

Around the same time, von Braun also made an impression on Captain Walter R. Dornberger. Dornberger was in charge of rocket research and

STELLAR!

As a young student, von Braun enjoyed reading science fiction. He even experimented with writing his own stories about space travel! His short story "Little Moon" was published in his school's magazine.

Dornberger (*second from left*) and von Braun (*second from right*) worked together at the Peenemünde research center.

development with the German army. He learned of von Braun's talents and saw **potential** in the young student.

Von Braun earned a **bachelor's degree** in mechanical engineering in 1932. Dornberger then arranged for von Braun to work with him at the army's rocket test facilities near Berlin.

4 Making Missiles

Though von Braun went to work for the army, he also continued his studies. In 1934, he received a **PhD** in **physics** from the University of Berlin. By this time, von Braun's research team had successfully developed and launched two rockets. The rockets traveled more than 1.5 miles (2.4 km) vertically into the air!

However, while von Braun dreamed of space travel, others dreamed of darker ways to use rocket **technology**. By 1934, Adolf Hitler had risen to power and was ruling Germany. He forbade rocket tests in the country except for military use. If von Braun wished to continue with rocket research, he would have to serve the **Nazi** army.

In 1939, **World War II** broke out across Europe. Military research was important to the war effort. A large research center was established in Peenemünde, on Germany's northern coast. Von Braun moved there with many other scientists in the early 1940s to continue his research. He was named technical director of the center.

Von Braun led a team in developing an A-4 **ballistic missile**. This rocket was later named the V-2. The V-2 used a liquid fuel

propellant that boosted it higher than anything that had come before.

Hitler believed rockets could be vital to winning the war. The **Allies** heard of Germany's developments in rocket **technology**. Leaders of these nations grew concerned. In August of 1943, Britain's Royal Air Force sent 600 bombers to destroy the Peenemünde research center.

The center was heavily damaged, but the bombs missed many of the most important buildings. Plans and drawings remained

The V-2 missile in Peenemünde. The research center there was turned into a museum.

intact. Hitler moved what was left of the facility near the town of Nordhausen, Germany.

The new facility was called Mittelwerk. Production of the V-2 continued there as planned. But now, development was done underground for improved security. Von Braun continued to play a leading role in **missile** development.

The first German attacks using the new missiles occurred in September 1944. France, Britain, and Belgium were all heavily bombarded. One attack on Britain killed around 3,000 people and injured thousands more.

Von Braun's work during the war is **controversial**. His leadership in developing the V-2 led to thousands of deaths. Von Braun argued afterward that there was little he could do. He cared deeply about his work and wished to develop his skills as a scientist. Living in Germany at the time, his only legal career option was to work for the **Nazi** Party. Protesting Nazi conduct would have put his career, and perhaps his life, in danger.

Von Braun enjoyed the study of many space topics, including astronomy.
But helping humans achieve spaceflight was always his main interest.

5 After War

As the war drew to a close in 1945, it became clear Germany would be defeated. **Allied** forces began arresting war criminals in German lands. Von Braun and other scientists fled to southern Germany, afraid of being pursued and captured for their involvement in war efforts.

The Allies were pursuing Germany's chief scientists, but not to arrest them. The search occurred at an important point in history. The United States and the Soviet Union were allies during **World War II**. But **tensions** formed between the two countries after 1945. This tension became known as the **Cold War**.

During the Cold War, the United States and Soviet Union competed to have the best **technology**. By the end of the war, German rocket and **missile** technology was the best in the world. The United States and Soviet Union raced to be the first to find Germany's advanced weapons and the scientists who built them.

Both countries hoped the scientists would help their nation develop these technologies outside of Germany. Von Braun's

talents had made him well-known. He was a key focus of this search.

In 1945, US troops found von Braun and his team in the Alps. The German scientists surrendered. Within a few months, von Braun was transported to the United States. He would live and work there for the rest of his life.

Von Braun was a US Army scientist for 15 years.

Project Paperclip

Upon arrival in the United States, von Braun and a group of about 125 other scientists were sent to Fort Bliss, Texas. There, many were part of a secret military operation called Project Paperclip. It involved overseeing tests on captured V-2 **missiles**. The German scientists were also instructed to teach American engineers about rocket **technology**.

Project Paperclip wasn't the only thing the US military kept secret. It kept the German scientists' presence in the United

States secret as well. **Nazi** actions during the war had greatly angered and upset citizens of the world. Not all Germans had been Nazis. But many people worldwide believed all Germans were. Because of this, the US government felt Americans would be upset about German scientists living in the United States.

The secrecy made von Braun's first year in the United States **frustrating** for him. He later stated that he and his team had felt like "distrusted aliens" in a "foreign land." However, von Braun also recognized the career opportunities living in the United States provided. Though frustrated at first, he was also happy to be in the country.

Project Paperclip involved many German scientists in addition to von Braun (*circled*).

17

7 Space Race

In December 1946, word got out about von Braun's US residence. The *El Paso Times* newspaper ran an article on him and his team! Some Americans were unhappy about the German scientists' residency. But others were interested in the scientists.

Von Braun was invited to speak at an El Paso Rotary Club event in January 1947. He spoke of his ambitions for space exploration. The speech impressed many listeners. Newspapers and magazines took an interest in the German scientists at Fort Bliss. Von Braun was on his way to becoming a celebrity of the space age.

In 1950, von Braun was moved to the Redstone Arsenal military base in Alabama. Two years later, he was promoted to **technical** director of the US Army's **ballistic missile** program.

As von Braun settled into his new life, the **Cold War** continued. **Tensions** between the United States and the Soviet Union led to a battle to dominate space exploration. This **era** became known as the "Space Race."

Both countries competed to be first to send a **satellite** into space. By now, von Braun had established himself as a talented

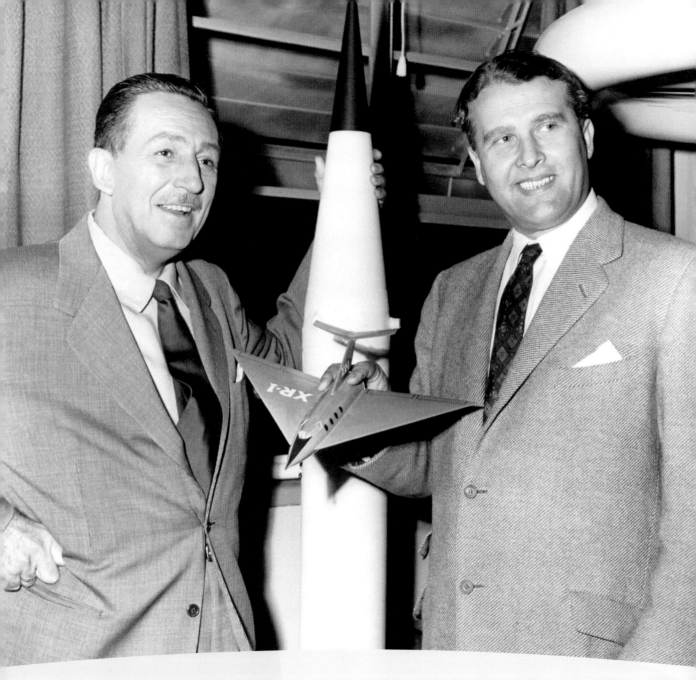

In the early years of the Space Race, Walt Disney (*left*) hired von Braun (*right*) to help produce three Disney films about space exploration.

leader and scientist. He designed a launch plan and presented it to the US government in 1954. Von Braun named the plan "Project Orbiter."

As von Braun and his team worked on launching a spacecraft, so did Soviet engineers. On October 4, 1957, the Soviet Union successfully launched a **satellite** into orbit! The Soviet satellite was called *Sputnik*. It was the world's first human-made satellite.

US scientists hurried to catch up with the Soviets. Von Braun worked to improve Project Orbiter. In January 1958, the US launched its own satellite, named *Explorer 1*.

Von Braun led the team behind *Explorer 1*'s journey to the stars. The satellite's successful launch led to a career change for him. In 1960, von Braun went to work for **NASA** as director of the future Marshall Space Flight Center.

The success of *Explorer 1* also put added pressure on the United States. US scientists worked hard to beat the Soviet Union in the next leg of the Space Race. But it seemed they could not catch up. On April 12, 1961, the Soviet Union launched the first person in history into space. But the race was close! The United States was not far behind from doing the same.

Von Braun (*right*) holds up a model of *Explorer 1* with US scientists who helped him develop the satellite.

8 Moon Mission

On May 5, 1961, **NASA** sent the first US astronaut, Alan Shepard, into space. US President John F. Kennedy challenged NASA to send a human to the moon by 1970. Von Braun embraced the challenge. Throughout the 1960s, he set his mind to developing new rockets that could reach the moon.

To get to the moon, space rockets would need more power than ever. Von Braun was in charge of developing a new series of super booster rockets called the Saturn series. These included the *Saturn I*, the *Saturn IB*, and the *Saturn V* models.

NASA began its Apollo program to prepare for and work toward a moon landing. Von Braun's *Saturn V* was used in several Apollo missions. These included the Apollo 4 mission in 1967 and the Apollo 6 mission in 1968. These were test missions launched without crews.

By 1969, the Apollo 11 mission was in the works. But this Apollo mission was not a test! NASA planned for it to carry a crew to the moon. And it would use von Braun's *Saturn V* to get them there.

STELLAR!
The *Saturn V* remains the world's tallest, heaviest, and most powerful rocket ever to operate.

Von Braun (*center*) describes the *Saturn V* launch system to President John F. Kennedy (*right*) in 1963.

The Apollo 11 launch took place on July 16, 1969. Four days later, millions of people watched a member of the Apollo 11 crew take his first step onto the moon. **NASA** cameras recorded the moonwalk and the footage was aired on national television!

The United States had finally bested the Soviet Union in space exploration.

After the moon landing, von Braun worked at **NASA** for another three years. He then took a job as president of **aerospace** company Fairchild Industries. In 1975, he founded the National Space Institute. This organization aimed to promote public understanding and support of space activities.

In 1976, US President Gerald Ford announced von Braun had earned the National Medal of Science. Unfortunately, von Braun had been diagnosed with **cancer** and was hospitalized. He could not accept the award in person at the time.

So, in January 1977, Vice President Nelson Rockefeller presented the award to von Braun in his hospital room. After accepting the award, von Braun said, "Here I have come in from another country and they give me this wonderful honor. Isn't this a wonderful country."

Von Braun died on June 16, 1977, at age 65. He had begun his life in the United States as a secret resident. By the time of his death, he had become one of the nation's best-known scientists.

Space Squad
APOLLO TASK FORCE

GEORGE MUELLER (1918–2015)

+ Engineer and leader of NASA's spaceflight programs

+ Program manager responsible for keeping the team on schedule

THOMAS KELLY (1929–2002)

+ Engineer

+ Led the team that developed the lunar module vehicle *Eagle*. The *Eagle* allowed Apollo 11 astronauts to travel to and from the moon's surface

MARGARET HAMILTON (1936–)

+ Computer scientist

+ Developed software that computed the moon landing. This programming provided the building blocks for modern software engineering

KATHERINE JOHNSON (1918–)

+ Mathematician

+ Calculated the trajectories of NASA spacecraft to prepare for the Apollo 11 moon landing

9 A Lasting Legacy

Von Braun's leading role in the moon landing sealed his place in history. But his dark past and involvement with **Nazi** Germany plagued him throughout his life.

By 1971, it had been almost 30 years since **World War II** ended. But people still questioned von Braun's past work for the Nazi Party. That year, von Braun received a letter from American Alan Fox. In the letter, Fox asked why von Braun did not protest Nazi conduct during the war.

Von Braun wrote Fox a long and sincere reply. Von Braun explained that he had not fully known how terrible Nazi conduct was and had never been interested in politics. He also explained that in times of war, his instinct was to do what he could to protect his country.

Despite this **controversy**, von Braun is remembered as a natural leader and ambitious scientist. He devoted much of his life to space exploration. His dreams had never been of weapons or destruction, but of helping humans explore the skies.

STELLAR!
Von Braun was called the "Moon Rocket King" and "Father of the American Space Age."

In 1970, Huntsville named February 24 "Wernher von Braun Day." Von Braun and his family were present to celebrate the honor.

When von Braun died, people across the world mourned him. Von Braun's contributions to rocket **technology** allowed humans to step foot on the moon. His achievements sparked the imaginations of a generation of scientists, space explorers, and dreamers.

Timeline

Wernher Von Braun is born on March 23 in Wirsitz, Germany.

1912

Von Braun graduates from the Berlin Institute of Technology with a bachelor's degree in mechanical engineering.

1932

Von Braun receives his PhD in physics from the University of Berlin.

1934

Germans launch the first attacks using von Braun's V-2 rocket missiles.

1944

1924
Wernher stages his first rocket experiment by tying store-bought rockets to his family's wagon.

1945
US troops transport von Braun to the United States, where he begins working on Project Paperclip.

The United
States
launches
satellite
Explorer 1.

1958

Von Braun's
Saturn V
rocket
launches into
space for
the Apollo 11
moon landing.

1969

President
Ford awards
von Braun
the National
Medal of
Science.

1976

1952
Von Braun
is promoted
to technical
director of
the US Army's
ballistic
missile
program.

1960
Von Braun
begins
working for
NASA.

1975
Von Braun
founds the
National
Space
Institute.

1977
Von Braun
dies of cancer
on June 16
at age 65.

Glossary

aerospace (EHR-oh-spays)—the space containing Earth's atmosphere and beyond. It is where rockets, satellites, and other spacecraft operate.

ally—people, groups, or nations united for some special purpose. During World War II Great Britain, France, the United States, and the Soviet Union were called the Allies.

bachelor's degree—a college degree that is usually earned after four years of study.

ballistic missile—a weapon guided upward in a steeply curving path before falling freely.

boarding school—a school that students may live in during the year.

cancer—any of a group of often deadly diseases marked by harmful changes in the normal growth of cells. Cancer can spread and destroy healthy tissues and organs.

Cold War—a period of tension and hostility between the United States and its allies and the Soviet Union and its allies after World War II.

confirm—to perform a ceremony admitting a person into a church.

controversial—of or relating to a discussion marked by strongly different views. Such a discussion is a controversy.

enroll—to register, especially in order to attend a school.

era—a period of time or history.

frustrate—to cause to feel upset, angry, or discouraged.

grant—a gift of money to be used for a special purpose.

intact—not broken or damaged.

interplanetary—existing, carried on, or operating between planets.

missile—a weapon that is thrown or projected to hit a target.

NASA—National Aeronautics and Space Administration. NASA is a US government agency that manages the nation's space program and conducts flight research.

Nazi—the political party that controlled Germany under Adolf Hitler from 1933 to 1945. Members of this party were called Nazis.

PhD—doctor of philosophy. Usually, this is the highest degree a student can earn.

physics—a science that studies matter and energy and how they interact.

potential—what a person is capable of achieving in the future.

propel—to drive forward or onward by some force. Something, such as fuel, that causes something to move forward is a propellant.

satellite—a manufactured object that orbits Earth. It relays scientific information back to Earth.

technology (tehk-NAH-luh-jee)—machinery and equipment developed for practical purposes using scientific principles and engineering. Something related to technology is technical.

tension—stress, nervousness, or difficulty between two persons or entities.

World War II—from 1939 to 1945, fought in Europe, Asia, and Africa. Great Britain, France, the United States, the Soviet Union, and their allies were on one side. Germany, Italy, Japan, and their allies were on the other side.

Index

A
awards, 24

B
ballistic missiles, 10, 11,
  12, 14, 16, 18
Berlin Institute of
  Technology, 8
bombings, 11, 12

C
Cold War, 14, 18

D
death, 24, 27
Dornberger, Walter R.,
  8, 9

E
education, 6, 8, 9, 10
Explorer 1, 20

F
family, 6
Ford, Gerald, 24

G
Germany, 4, 6, 8, 9, 10, 11,
  12, 14, 26

H
Hitler, Adolf, 10, 11, 12

M
moon landing, 4, 22, 23,
  24, 25, 26, 27

N
NASA, 20, 22, 23, 24, 25
National Space Institute,
  24
Nazi Party, 4, 10, 12, 17,
  26

O
Oberth, Hermann, 6, 8

P
Peenemünde research
  center, 10, 11
public speaking, 18

R
Rockefeller, Nelson, 24
*Rocket into
  Interplanetary Space,
  The*, 6
rocket technology, 4, 8, 9,
  10, 11, 14, 16, 22, 27

S
Saturn V, 4, 22
Shepard, Alan, 22
Soviet Union, 14, 18, 20,
  24
Space Race, 18, 20
Sputnik, 20

T
Texas, 16

U
University of Berlin, 10

W
World War II, 4, 10, 11, 12,
  14, 17, 26